Self-Love

30 Day Self-Love Challenge; Build your Self-Confidence and Self-Esteem Through Unconditional Self Love

© **Copyright 2016 -**_____ **All rights reserved.**

This document is geared towards providing exact and reliable information in regards to the topic and issue covered. The publication is sold on the idea that the publisher is not required to render accounting, officially permitted, or otherwise, qualified services. If advice is necessary, legal or professional, a practiced individual in the profession should be ordered.

- From a Declaration of Principles which was accepted and approved equally by a Committee of the American Bar Association and a Committee of Publishers and Associations.

In no way is it legal to reproduce, duplicate, or transmit any part of this document by either electronic means or in printed format. Recording of this publication is strictly prohibited and any storage of this document is not allowed unless with written permission from the publisher. All rights reserved.

The information provided herein is stated to be truthful and consistent, in that any liability, in terms of inattention or otherwise, by any usage or abuse of any policies, processes, or directions contained within is the solitary and utter responsibility of the recipient reader. Under no circumstances will any legal responsibility or blame be held against the publisher for any reparation, damages, or monetary loss due to the information herein, either directly or indirectly.

Respective authors own all copyrights not held by the publisher.

The information herein is offered for informational purposes solely and is universal as so. The presentation of the information is without contract or any type of guarantee assurance.

The trademarks that are used are without any consent, and the publication of the trademark is without permission or backing by the trademark owner. All trademarks and brands within this book are for clarifying purposes only and are the owned by the owners themselves, not affiliated with this document.

Free membership into the Mastermind Self Development Group!

For a limited time, you can join the Mastermind Self Development Group for free! You will receive videos and articles from top authorities in self development as well as a special group only offers on new books and training programs. There will also be a monthly member only draw that gives you a chance to win any book from your Kindle wish list!

If you sign up through this link http://www.mastermindselfdevelopment.com/specialreport you will also get a special free report on the Wheel of Life. This report will give you a visual look at your current life and then take you through a series of exercises that will help you plan what your perfect life looks like. The workbook does not end there; we then take you through a process to help you plan how to achieve that perfect life. The process is very powerful and has the potential to change your life forever. Join the group now and start to change your life! http://www.mastermindselfdevelopment.com/specialreport

Table of Contents

Introduction

Phase 1 – The Person You Are Now –
Chapter 1 – Days 1 to 5
Day 1 – Establish where you are now
Day 2 – Start on your journey of self-discovery
Day 3 – Making a date with yourself
Day 4 – Feed yourself positivity
Day 5 – Recognizing your own abilities

Phase 2 – Adding Value to Who You Are
Chapter 2 – Days 6 – 16
Applying the 80/20 principle to your life
Looking at friendships
Chapter 3 – Days 17 to 20

Phase 3 – Finding the Authentic You
Chapter 4 – Days 21 to 25

Phase 4 – Letting the Butterfly Emerge
Chapter 5 – Day 26-30
Choose a venue
Do the mirror test
Read up on what's happening in the world or in the area
Handling social criticism

Conclusion

Introduction

I bet you didn't know that the amount of love you feel for yourself determines the amount of love other people feel for you. It's perfectly true. Think about it. If you don't like yourself very much, how much could you expect people to like you? The problem is that you have been fed all kinds of information during your life. You may have been told not to be selfish and may have interpreted that as not allowing yourself any kind of personal freedom. However, the truth is that selfishness and self-love are two very separate things.

The other background information which you may use to determine your lifestyle is feedback from others. If you were the most unpopular kid in school, it's hard to like yourself, knowing that all your peers disliked you. Society places labels on people. You could have been the "fat" kid. You could have been the "geek" but the truth is that, regardless of these labels, if you love who you are, all the negativity that surrounds you disappears because people respect you. Your self-respect demands that you surround yourself with people who do that. It follows that you need to examine what's making you so unhappy about yourself.

In this book, we teach you in four phases that make up the 30 day period in which you can expect to see changes. We look at your past. We look at the things you want to happen in your life. We look at the way that you see yourself. Together – you as a reader and me as a writer – will discover what makes you tick and what stops the clock from ticking midstream and makes you dislike who you are.

The steps are simple but you need to be serious about wanting to be happier. Of course, you may say that everyone wants to be happy, but the problem with that theory is that unhappy people tend to stay in that space until they are jolted out of it. This book is intended to give you the jolt that you need because you are worth it. By reading through the pages, you will be able to see problems that face you and learn how to move on from them – improving your sense of self-worth until you have no doubt about who you are. You will respect who you are and what you will notice is that people around you are starting to treat you in a more respectful way. Not only that, you will increase your chances to fulfill your dreams and to encourage positive interaction with people that gives each of you equal value.

Phase 1 – The Person You Are Now –

Chapter 1 – Days 1 to 5

How your past affects who you are depends on how your parents treated you or how you learned more about yourself from your peers. Unfortunately, children can be very cruel. Perhaps you didn't meet up to their standards for some reason and they were unkind to you. You don't understand it yet, but when people are cruel to you, it says much more about their insecurities than it does about yours. Similarly, parents who compare kids and make one kid feel useless are not that hot at parenting skills but they are good in passing blame to the child. What they fail to understand is that you can't compare children and expect them to be carbon copies of each other. If you believe that you are a failure because your parents have always reinforced that as fact, then you need to start looking at creating your own value in your own eyes and stop looking at your faults from their perspective. Phrases that come to mind are these:

- You will never amount to much
- You will never be as good as your brother/sister
- After all, we have done for you

These phrases are phrases that stick in your mind because they are very hurtful coming from people that matter. Although you may not have thought about them for a while, they are most certainly at the root of why you don't like yourself very much. Just as you were taught math and science, your parents or your siblings taught you who THEY believe you to be. You were young and impressionable and took it to heart and believed it to be true.

In this part of the experience, we want you to look at all the bad things that go through your mind about yourself. These are the things that affect your level of happiness and give you self-esteem issues. They may be related to your childhood. They may be related to relationships but wherever these negative messages are coming from, you need to recognize them so that we can work on them together to make you feel like you can overcome other people's approval of who you are.

Day 1 – Establish where you are now

Try to write down the things about yourself that make you unhappy and then look further and decide what events in your life confirmed this view of you. Was is what people said? Was it something you did? You need to see this clearly and the first exercise on the first day is to write that down because we are going to show you how to put all that self-doubt into the past and bring you up to speed with how to begin the journey into loving who you are. Don't think that this process will all be as negative as this. This is your first step toward happiness but you have a few hurdles to overcome before you can attain happiness. This self-discovery helps you to find a way out of the rut that you have become a part of.

Day 2 – Start on your journey of self-discovery

On the second day of your challenge, we want you to open that list and tear it up. Make a real ceremony of it. Celebrate letting go of all that negativity. What you are saying when you rip it up is:

I refuse to let my happiness be dictated by what other people think.
I am making a stand and today is a new beginning
I don't have to live in the past anymore. Today is the start of being myself

Don't expect to feel motivated straight away or expect to feel differently, but set the mood so that you are ready to make changes and to start embracing the happiness in life that is rightfully yours.

Dress up for work or whatever you are doing and put on your bravest face. If you dress in dowdy clothes, you feel worse about yourself, so try to choose something that you know looks nice on you and that makes you feel great inside. This is about who you ARE and you have the potential to become so much more, once we have been through the stages of letting go of negative thoughts.

Today you will learn to be happy on the surface. When thoughts come to your mind that make you doubt your own happiness, banish them and replace them with something else. Think of a song that makes you feel good and when these thoughts come into your mind, replace them with silent singing in your mind of the words of that song. This may seem a little banal but what you are doing is going through each moment of your day refusing to let the voice inside you tell you things that are negative. You are not yet at the stage where positive affirmations will work, so you need something else to have in your mind to use as an escape route from negativity.
Greet the world with a smile. Even if you must force that smile. Practice it in the mirror if you need to and make sure that the world sees your happy side. You won't see it yet. It's not going to cause miracles to happen, but what you see reflected from a smile is positivity from other people and that will help you in your plight to be happy.

Day 3 – Making a date with yourself

There's a wonderful book by Julia Cameron which is entitled "The Artist's Way" and which helps people to find their creativity. One element of the book is very useful to help you to become happier. In the mornings when you wake up, make sure that you give yourself sufficient time to do it because it will help your level of happiness. All you need is a diary and a pen placed by the side of the bed. When you wake up, take these first few moments as a date with yourself and without thinking of what you are saying, write down whatever comes to your mind. You are emptying your mind of anything that may be in it at the beginning of the day and thus starting your day with a fresh slate. You don't need to read or examine what you write. Simply write it and liberate your thoughts. Then put the book away.

Carry on the theme for the rest of the day by thinking of this day as a date. Dress up as if you had a date. Look at the day as a day of discovery because you need to know what makes you think in a positive way. Look nice, mix with people you like and who don't bring you down and if you don't have anyone in mind, go into town and sit in a street café and watch the world go by. Look out for people who are confident and happy and observe them. The concepts that are put into our minds by others are often very inaccurate. For example, if you are overweight and think this is the reason for your unhappiness, look at overweight people who appear to be happy. It's nonsense that you should feel unhappy because of something like this when so many people live with that problem and are happy. If you think you are too short, it's the same thing. Observe short people. Make yourself feel that who you are is perfectly normal and observe people being happy. Remember not to think negative thoughts and to greet people with a smile.

Day 4 – Feed yourself positivity

On this day, choose to do something that you love doing. It isn't going to be judged by anyone. Choose something YOU love. It may be watching a movie. It may be having a bath and playing with bubbles. It may be going to a football match or visiting an art gallery. Today you are going to be YOU. You are not going to let anyone else influence what you do and you are going to discover things that you like in life and begin to recognize the true nature of who you are. Don't think to yourself "what can I do that the other people would approve of" because it's not about other people. It's about who you are and amid all the confusion of life, unhappy people who don't love themselves have actually forgotten to measure themselves by their own standards of happiness. You need to start seeing what makes YOU happy and stop trying to please everyone else.

Day 5 – Recognizing your own abilities

Take pen to paper and write down all the things you can do. You may not think you can do much but during your life, you have gone through learning stages and have learned how to do certain things. People who love themselves know what these things are while those who do not, tend to push these to the back of their minds and think they have achieved very little. Achieving can start from childhood. Are you able to walk? Are you able to drive? Did you ever paint a picture? Can you cook? Are you good at wallpapering? Are you able to write poetry? You need to write down all the things you are good at. You are not doing this to impress anyone. You don't need to exaggerate. In fact, it's best that you don't. After each phrase, write down a qualifier, as follows:

I am good at cooking – I learned to cook because I love good food.
I am a great dancer – I am good at dancing because I practiced a lot.
I am a good driver – I am good at driving because I have good powers of observation.

Over these last five days, the object of the exercise is to work with what you are now so that you can expand upon those things you recognize as being part of who you are and make like much happier and fulfilling. You should continue to greet the world with a smile and use your song to silent bad thoughts. People are not drawn toward miserable people. Thus, your smile should act like a magnet to attract positive people. If you want someone to love you, you must first learn self-love. To offer someone less than that you deny yourself the chance of true happiness. Would you want someone who wasn't whole and who didn't like who he/she was? A more valuable relationship can happen when you respect yourself and love who you are because it makes you more complete. For the time being, go through the motions. Things are about to change.

Phase 2 – Adding Value to Who You Are
Chapter 2 – Days 6 – 16

Over the course of the next ten days, we are going to introduce you to ways to increase your level of self-love. Do you remember writing out a list of the things that you can do? Take it into your hand and look through it. Decide which activities give you the most pleasure. It may be cooking. It may be cycling or swimming. It may be playing games on your computer. Which of the activities really make you enthusiastic about life? You should ideally choose activities that can involve other people because you need to gradually introduce positive encounters with others into your life. For example, if you like cooking, that's a great start. Let's show you what I mean:

I can cook well – Make a cake for an elderly neighbor and give it to her.
I like driving – Drive to somewhere inspirational with a positive friend.
I like painting pictures – Join an art class so you can paint pictures with others who enjoy the same thing.
I am good at looking after animals – Go to the local pet shelter and see if you can offer a little bit of help with the animals.
I like watching movies – Pick a positive friend and ask if he/she would like to share a movie. Make it an event with popcorn and laughter.

You already know that these are activities you are good at so they will generally be things that you feel happy about. People enjoy self-achievement. Thus, what you are doing is building events into those things that you are good at but offering another thing that helps you to feel good about who you are. Volunteerism really does work well as does mixing with people who have like interests. In the case of baking a cake for an elderly neighbor or helping with a pet shelter, you don't have to commit more time than you want and can choose your level of commitment. A cake takes an hour or so to bake and then you will need about an hour for that visit. You are not simply giving the neighbor the cake and then walking away. If you are invited in, give a little of your time to that elderly person and think of it as your good deed for the day. Don't expect anything in return. People make the mistake of looking for approval and you may just catch that neighbor on a day when she is troubled so if you expect nothing, you don't leave yourself open to disappointment.

Now look at things that make you happy. Close your eyes and imagine a time in your life when you were happy and smiling. Try to picture it and find out what it was that day that made your life so happy. Try not to center it upon people unless those people are still around and still in your life. You can't wish that things could go back to how they were, but you can foster those friendships that are still potentials. If there was a person in your thoughts, give them a ring and be positive. Make the phone call about them rather than about you. When you give unconditionally, you are not laying any trip upon someone and you are not going to be disappointed with them. Expect nothing. Just let that person know you were thinking about him/her.

Applying the 80/20 principle to your life

This principle may be something you are unfamiliar with. What an Italian, called Vilfredo Pareto discovered was that 80 percent of the Italian population worked hard but that those who gained the most from that work were the 20 percent who were rich. This principle can be applied to any area of life. For example, 20 percent of the time you are happy but 80 percent of the time you go through the motions and are not that happy. This was a wonderful discovery because it demonstrated that if you can level out the percentages between being happy and not being happy, your life becomes more fulfilled. In your case, you need more self-esteem, so you need to up the percentage of time you feel happy about who you are.

Then look at what things give you real pleasure. What makes your eyes light up with joy? What gives you a passion for life? Maybe you love the coastline. Maybe you feel at home there and enjoy being close to nature. Chances are that you don't do whatever it is that much so you need to up the enjoyment factor in your life. Make a point of increasing the percentage of time you feel happy and comfortable with yourself and what you are doing. These positive experiences help you to be happier with yourself and to respect yourself more. It's something YOU love. It's personal and you need to apply it more often in your life to up the percentage of joy you allow yourself to enjoy.

Looking at friendships

During this ten days, write down a list of the people who are currently in your life. Next to each of them, give them points based on the following criteria. Does that person contribute to your life in a positive way? Does that person make you feel happy? Does that person make you feel worse about yourself? Does that person use you? Does that person respect or love you? Does that person make you feel good about yourself?

What you are doing is assessing your friendships and your relationships with family and friends and finding out which of your friends approve of and accept who you are and which make you feel bad about yourself. There is a thing called "toxic friendships" and these are the ones that belittle you or make you feel like you don't measure up. You need to decide which category each of these people belong in and cut ties with anyone who makes you feel negative about yourself. That's not friendship and the more you mix with people like this, the less likely you are to love yourself. Perhaps there will be a time when you have room for these people in your life, but it must be on your terms and that is strictly give and take in equal proportions.

Now look at the names of people who are positive and friendly and make you feel good about yourself. These are friendships you need to keep going and perhaps when you felt down about life, you haven't been in touch with them much. Mend the bridges and call them, but remember it's not about your own dramas. It is about them. If you want to keep friendships on a give and take basis, you need to give especially if you haven't been in touch for a while. Don't make demands of them. Simply inquire how they are and talk about things that are positive in your relationship with them. Catch up on their news and if they need a little extra support because they are going through tough times, give that support because these are people you chose as being positive influences. Volunteering to help them won't harm your potential to love yourself because you will be doing something good for someone you know to deserve it.

All of the time that you are adding to the percentage of time spent pleasurably, you are adding positivity to your life. Remember, smile at the world and it will smile back. Stop feeling like you don't measure up because when you think in this way, it is you who defines the measurement of your own usefulness. If you don't measure up, don't think about it. Do something that helps you to measure up. In this phase, what you are doing is making sure that maximize opportunities to be with positive people, to do things that you enjoy without pressure from others and use your skills to create positive experiences that can include others in a positive way. You owe yourself that much and it you owe it to the people who play a very positive part in your life.

You are halfway done!

Congratulations on making it to the halfway point of the journey. Many try and give up long before even getting to this point, so you are to be congratulated on this. You have shown that you are serious about getting better every day. I am also serious about improving my life, and helping others get better along the way. To do this I need your feedback. Click on the link below and take a moment to let me know how this book has helped you. If you feel there is something missing or something you would like to see differently, I would love to know about it. I want to ensure that as you and I improve, this book continues to improve as well. Thank you for taking the time to ensure that we are all getting the most from each other.

http://viewbook.at/selflove

Chapter 3 – Days 17 to 20

So far you have learned to make the pleasurable part of your life more rewarding so that it overshadows the negative parts of your life. This makes you like your life more and thus like yourself a little more than you used to. Self-love goes a little bit further than that and in this four days, we are going to delve into the kind of things you can do to improve the way you see yourself.

Katy was a person who didn't like herself very much. She went through life thinking that this was normal. In fact, she dated and eventually got married, but there was still something missing in her life. When we talked together, what was obvious was that Katy didn't really like herself much at all. She believed that the abusive husband she had been married to was all she deserved. The problem with this way of thinking is that you reinforce your own lack of value. When he did things that hurt her, he knew exactly what he was doing. He was a manipulator. He knew that as long as she felt she was to blame, she would never leave him and in fact, Katy explained how she felt powerless to leave. It had taken a particularly violent event to make her leave because she dreaded the consequences of staying more than the consequences of leaving and believed that one day, she would not get over his violent abuse. Katy went from this relationship into an equally abusive relationship, still feeling it was all she deserved. This time, the abuse was emotional. The relationship did not last and she came for help because she couldn't understand that her life was a series of abusive relationships because she had not yet learned to love herself. It took a lot of work to get her to see the positive side of who she was, but when she did, she realized she didn't have to be this non-assertive person with no self-respect. She learned to increase the amount of things she did that gave HER pleasure. She learned to up her self-esteem by volunteering to work at an animal shelter and when she became whole as a person found a wonderful husband because a positive person with self-love and respect tends to attract people who are looking for an equal partner, rather than one who wants to dominate.

Katy recalled all the years that had made her life seem so miserable and now looks back upon it realizing that she herself contributed to her own misery. It wasn't that she wasn't worthy. It was that she took too much lead from people who made her feel unworthy. That's when self-love failed and she became the person people said she was instead of letting her true personality shine.

I give you this example for a purpose. Katy wasn't taking ownership of her own life or her own destination in life. She wasn't taking responsibility for who she was. She was quick to blame others when the blame rested with her for allowing people to kill all love she may otherwise have felt for herself. When you don't feel self-love and respect, you don't expect people around you to treat you with respect, so it's important that you become a valued human being who can show the world that you have respect for yourself.

In this next 5 days, I want you to employ something called mindfulness. Remember to smile at the world. Remember to keep to all the lessons we have already given you, but on top of this, I need you to sit silently once a day and observe what's happening around you. Look at the changing color of the leaves on the trees. Look at the color of the sky. Be in that moment. What this means is that as you sit there, if thoughts come into your head, you simply dismiss them and come back into this moment. The way mindfulness works is that it dismisses all the things that have passed because they are gone and you can do nothing to change them. It cuts out worries about the future. The future hasn't happened yet so it doesn't count. In these fifteen to twenty minutes a day, concentrate on the now. Breathe in through your nostrils and hold the breath for a moment and then breathe out. Be conscious of the breath. See it like a fire going into your body to warm it and then let it go. Thoughts will come and go and as they do, make no judgment on them. Don't let them hurt you. Just think of them as puffs of smoke and watch as they disappear. Don't judge those thoughts or waste emotions on them. They are simply what they are – thoughts that take no real tangible form unless YOU let them. They don't lead to sentimental thought because you stop the process by dismissing them. They don't lead to tears because you don't add any kind of sentiment to them. They are just clouds of smoke that you allow to pass through your head and then dismiss.

The value that you are adding to your life by doing this is that you are refusing to be brought down by thoughts. Thoughts can't hurt you if you treat them in this way and you can continue doing that every time negative thoughts come into your head. It's up to you whether you continue to think in a negative way or let those thoughts go. Katy learned to do this and found that instead of reinstating her lack of worth, she was adding to her sense of worth and that's what this exercise is all about.

Do the same thing when you are eating. Take your time and enjoy every flavor, texture, and taste instead of rushing it so you can get to the next task at hand. Slow your life down to a state where thoughts do not take precedence over what's real at this moment in time. When you do that, you begin to see all the wonders that life offers you and enjoy being part of it.

Phase 3 – Finding the Authentic You
Chapter 4 – Days 21 to 25

If you have self-esteem problems or don't like yourself very much, chances are that you live your life dominated by other people's thoughts – or at least you think you do. When Mike went about his daily life, he found there wasn't much of himself in those days. There were obligations to others. He even found that he watched TV programs that other people liked. He ate what other people insisted he ate and he didn't seem to have anything in his life that was his choice. If you put your own dreams on hold all the time, you can't find the authentic you because you are letting other people decide what that is. Mike would listen to his wife's music. He would fit his life in with others, rather than allow himself any kind of personal freedom and you need that freedom to be able to find joy.

We taught him how to introduce ideas that were his. We taught him how to decide for himself what he wanted to do. Of course, there are going to be obligations. You must work. You must do housework. You must eat, but he started to assert his choices and let the people around him know who he was instead of always putting up with the things that everyone else wanted. When it came to vacations, he told his wife he hated the beach and they decided to take separate vacations so that they could both do what they wanted to do. When she watched TV and the program was not interesting for him, he went to another room and did what he wanted to do. He started to realize that the authentic Mike was there all the time, but that he had let it be dominated by the needs and wants of other people.

When you wake up on each of the five days, be conscious of what you do and what you want to do. If you normally have cereal for breakfast, is that what you want or is it just for convenience? If you want a tropical fruit cocktail or fancy a piece of toast, have it. Stop limiting the scope of your imagination and letting time dictate to you what you have. Throughout the day, look at all the choices you make and see if they are your choices or the choices of someone else. For example, at lunchtime, do you carry on working? Explain to your boss that you need to do something at lunchtime and go out into the fresh air or go window shopping – whatever pleases you.

So far in life, you are letting other people decide who you are and it's time to decide for yourself who you are. If you live alone, look at your routines. Look at the things you feel obliged to do and see if you can switch them out for things you prefer to do. You need to tidy up what is authentically you and what is imposed upon you.

When Angela got home every night, she sat down and looked at the photos of her ex-husband and almost sought his approval. He had left her. He wasn't coming back but still she looked at those photographs that hurt her and allowed that hurt to part of her life, even though he was living a great life with another woman. Pack away the souvenirs – especially the ones that make you into a person you are not anymore. Stop wallowing in it and get on with finding out who YOU are, rather than thinking about who you should have been. Stop digging into the past for reasons. If you do that, you deny yourself the chance of liking yourself. If you surround yourself with souvenirs of someone who doesn't love you anymore, you give yourself a reason to dislike yourself. He doesn't have the right to be in your life anymore. Even if you don't want to throw away the photos, put them in a box in the attic where they belong and start to live your life.

During these days, do not feel committed to do things for other people that you really don't have the time to do. When you have no sense of self, you tend to do that. People ask you to babysit and you go, even though you don't really want to. Learn to be authentic. Be real about what you want to do. Tell them "I can't babysit tonight. I have other plans." Stop being a doormat for people and find your own things to do. Sit back and enjoy your absolute favorite movie or music and make sure it's not something you listen to or watch because it reminds you of someone and makes you wish he/she was back in your life. Decide for yourself. It doesn't matter about the past. It doesn't matter about the future. The other thing that matters right now is YOU. Janet listened to classical music because of the influence of her last love. She had learned to listen to it to gain his approval of who she was and certain pieces of classical music were too complex for her to enjoy. She went through all the CDs that she had and she eliminated his choices from her life.

Alice did the same. After her husband died, she suddenly faced this feeling that she didn't know which of the choices in her life were hers and which had been inflicted upon her. She had been married for so many years that she had somehow lost who she was and didn't think she could cope without him. She went through all the possessions, the friendships and the things that they had done together and decided to make a list of all of the elements that made up her life. By crossing off things that really didn't give her any joy, she found time to do things that she had always wanted to do.

Start, within these days, to give yourself that extra space for joy. The authentic you is the person that is happy with your own choices. You are entitled to your opinions and they count as much as anyone else's does, regardless of what you may have believed up until this moment in time. Try to make a list of things that you want to do in your life. This isn't a life changing bucket list of the impossible, but a list of things that you can do at home that you never found the time for.

Carol did this and what she found she enjoyed doing most was reading. Her life never seemed to allow her enough time to read. She found that she could allow herself that time to read by giving up on things that were being inflicted on her. For example, she always got her neighbor's kids come over in the evenings and although it was pleasurable at first, it meant that she had very little time to herself. She decided that the neighbor needed to find someone else to share the load. Just because she was single and she was there didn't mean she had to burden herself with her neighbor's problems every day of her life. In fact, when she told the neighbor she needed more time alone, the neighbor responded that she was surprised that it had lasted this long!

You must write down things that are important to you and that make up part of who you are. Here is a list to show you the kind of examples and how to then put them into your life to replace things that are not authentically you.

I want to paint pictures – I am too busy with the resident's committee obligations.
Solution: Cut down the resident's committee obligations. You don't like them anyway and there is always someone else that will take your place. Your life is passing too quickly to do things that don't give you joy. Let those obligations gives someone else joy!

I want to go on a Buddhist retreat – I don't have time.
Solution: Find out about the Buddhist retreat. Find out what it costs, and start to put money aside. Find out what vacation you are due and work toward it, even if it means getting a part time job just until you have enough to do what it is you want to do.

I want to live in a nicer house – Your house is probably not as bad as you think it is, and before you decide about doing something drastic, how about cleaning up the space you have and feeling the liberation of letting go of possessions. Then you can decide based on a tidy house if this is something you really want. Get rid of things that don't give you joy. Free up your home to incorporate your own style. Make it feel like your own.

I want to play a musical instrument – Liz started playing the guitar at 62. She became very good at it. If you really want to do it, do it. You don't have to buy a grand piano or make the dream so large that you can't achieve it. Start with something relatively small and work your way to the dream.

As a second exercise in this phase, sit down and close your eyes whenever you feel that your life is miserable or whenever you feel you are not good enough. Think of things that give you joy. Maybe it's as simple as an ice cream. Maybe it's as complex as seeing yourself in a wonderful place in your life. If you ever saw the movie "Mrs. Harris goes to Paris" you will know that it's about an old lady who always wanted to wear a Dior dress.

So instead of telling herself it was impossible, she saved up all the money she earned as a cleaner and eventually went to Paris to buy that dress. Think of what your dreams and hopes are. Use moments of doubt to reinforce the ideas that you have put to one side all your life in favor of doing the necessary. You need dreams. You need goals and you need things that send your heart into a sense of authenticity to make you feel good about yourself.

Carol wanted to see her name in lights as an actress but didn't know where to start until she allowed that vision to become part of her everyday hopes. Noticing an advert in a local store, she joined the theater group and indeed starred in a local play. She didn't have to be a Hollywood star. She just wanted to enjoy acting and this allowed her to do that. You need to use these moments when you close your eyes to imagine the things that you want in your life. When I close mine, I think of boat rides on calm waters and I achieved that by living near a lake and now have the opportunity every day of my life of having that dream as part of my life. Dreams and hopes don't have to be so huge that you can't fulfill them. Find out what your AUTHENTIC dreams are and embrace them. Find a way to work toward them.

In this phase, it's important to know that people around you can only influence your choices if you let them. If you are asked to go see a movie that doesn't interest you, say so. Find an alternative that interests everyone. If you are pushed into doing things you don't want to do, ask yourself why you are doing them. Of course, there are exceptions to the rule. Sometimes you have obligations that you can't get out of, but the mistake comes when you insist on making those occasions part and parcel of your everyday life and let other people inflict their views upon you so much that you forget your own.

Be authentic. If that means changing a few things in your life, then do it. If you cannot be true to yourself, you begin to lose respect in who you are and tend to favor the views and obligations placed on you by others. Stop it. You have choices. People who don't love themselves allow others to make those choices. They step away from being responsible for their own happiness in doing so. Make your mark. Be authentic.

Phase 4 – Letting the Butterfly Emerge

Chapter 5 – Day 26-30

You have been on a journey of self-discovery. Now it's time to let that butterfly within you emerge and socialize with people showing a level of confidence you have never experienced before. You know how to get worries and insecurities out of your mind by using mindfulness. You know about mixing with positive people instead of those who bring you down. You also know that you are responsible for the person you are. Thus, over the course of the next few days, you are going to launch yourself onto the social scene and enjoy being who you are.

Choose a venue – You need to know where it is that you are going and organize it in advance. Perhaps you want to go to an art gallery opening or maybe to watch a carnival. Whatever it is that you want to do on this treat day must involve other people. You need to be mixing with folks who are positive and people you may not yet have met. You also need to feel comfortable with the situation so choose something that makes it easy for you to mix with people. During the time that you spend with people, watch out for doubts in your mind, take a mental note and then let go of them. Remember when we worked on mindfulness, the idea is to see these negative thoughts as something that doesn't affect you. Let go of them and feel comfortable.

For this event, make sure that you are aware of the dress code and take a pride in dressing yourself up for the event. Even if it's just meeting a couple of friends in a public place, dress appropriately and wear clothing that doesn't make you feel self-conscious. Carolyn tried this and wore impressive high heels and as soon as she arrived, she realized she could hardly walk in them. Don't make that kind of mistake. It is far better to arrive in comfortable shoes than to draw people's attention to you because you didn't prepare for the event.

The kind of events that are good for your "coming out" are family events, a local dance, a village picnic or something that really interests you. You may want to go to a reunion or meet up with people who used to be friends but that you have neglected. Avoid events that discourage talking to other people, such as the cinema or theater unless you have arranged to go for a meal with someone beforehand. Perhaps you could call up some people you feel guilty about not sharing enough time with. Maybe your sisters or brothers haven't been people you have spent much time with lately and you want to catch up with family news. Plan your event so that it's something that you enjoy and share it with people who you know will also enjoy your choice. There's not much point in making arrangements with reluctant people. Therefore, choose people whose interests fit the event you intend to invite them to.

Wear shoes that are comfortable and, as you dress for the event, approve of everything you wear from your underwear right through to the coat you choose. Make yourself look nice and feel nice inside. If you need to have your hair done for the event, program it so that you have enough time to wash your hair if you are disappointed with the style. Do nothing to make yourself feel bad. For example, don't wear clothing that is too tight simply because you are trying to conform to society's idea of what size you should be. Don't wear heels you can't walk in. Don't wear things to please others. This is all about you.

Do the mirror test

Place a full-length mirror where you can see yourself coming into a door. Go outside the room and then make your entry, observing things that may let you down. Body language is a terrible giveaway. If you are shy and nervous, you may find that you look downward as you enter the room or that your shoulders are not as straight as they should be. You almost cower. Your head needs to be straight so that your eyes meet those of people you are about to meet. Your shoulders should be straight and you should enter the room with a smile on your face. This isn't a huge smile. It's a polite smile of greeting. Try placing a seat in view of the mirror and enter the room and sit down and see how clumsily you do it. You are not trying to be anything other than who you are. You are merely trying to present yourself in the best light possible. Enter the room, greet others who are there and then sit down. Practice it in the mirror. Are your clothes still comfortable when you sit? If not, choose clothing that is.

If you find that your body has lumps and bumps where they should not be, chances are that you are wearing clothing a size too small. Often people do this when they don't want to admit to having grown a size, but if you feel that fussy about it, buy the larger sized underwear and take the labels out. Suddenly all those lumps and bumps disappear and it makes you look slimmer. Don't package yourself up to be something you are not. When you are authentic, you are relaxed with who you are and comfortable in the skin you're in.

Read up on what's happening in the world or in the area

Often people feel it's awkward to talk to others because they really don't know what to say. If you know what's happening in the news, this helps you to have something to say. Perhaps there was something that happened locally that you can discuss. Discussing the weather is a bit of a cop out and people use this sometimes to break the ice. It shows you as a confident person if you can the lead. Shake hands or greet those that you meet and be ready to observe. If they mention something, try to continue the conversation. If they don't, bring something up yourself as a natural progression, rather than blurting something out for the sake of it. Let's show you an example.

Other person: Good evening
You: Good evening. I am glad you could make it.
Other person: I am not sure I am going to be good company.
You: I am sure you will be.

What you are doing in this conversation is reassuring someone and making them feel comfortable in your presence. The person who says that they are not good company is sending signals. "I am not really good in company" and your reassurance helps that person to feel more at ease. Now try introducing something new into the conversation:

You: Did you see the news tonight?
Other person: No, I didn't have time. Anything interesting?
You: Yes. They are apparently going to build a new theater locally. That should be good."
Other person: I didn't know that. I will need to keep a lookout for news.

In this instance, you are telling someone about something that is happening locally that is relevant. Make your conversations relevant. You need to get over this thought that you are not good enough or that you don't have what it takes to mix with others. We all do and sometimes you need to help yourself a little socially to feel more comfortable. In fact, the more you mix with people, the easier it becomes. Small talk is used to break the ice. It's that initial contact with others. Hold your head up high. If someone mentions something you know nothing about, don't think of yourself as being stupid. Simply acknowledge that you know nothing about it. Stop trying to be someone you are not. The authentic you will have more pleasure than the one that pretends to live up to other people's standards. Be happy with who you are and show the world that you are happy to be entitled to your own opinions, being gracious always and appreciating that others are entitled to theirs.

Handling social criticism

When Sara took it upon herself to invite people around to her house for dinner, she knew that these were people likely to criticize her choices. She had suffered from a lack of self-love all her life but had gone through the process of change and was now happy about who she was. She knew that the people coming were partly responsible for the negative feelings she had fostered about who she was. This was the first event for her when they would have to accept her as she was.

At first, one of the guests muttered surprise at the choice of dress Sara had made and made some comment about the color not suiting her. Sara understood by now that people who criticize in this way do so because of their own insecurity. She had learned to be happy and authentic and didn't need other people's approval. Feeling empathy toward the woman who criticized her, she simply turned and changed the subject. "Your dress is lovely," she said. "Such a great color on you." The woman was taken aback and was not expecting this kind of retort. By deflecting the insult, Sara managed to get past the criticism and steer the conversation back onto something positive. It's quite easy to do and when you learn to be empathetic and put yourself in the shoes of others, you may find that they have less confidence and self-love than you do. By being kind, you can make a remark that adds positivity to the situation.

In another situation, Susan was criticized by her parents at one such dinner. Her mother disapprovingly made the comment "No sign of grandchildren yet then?" and Susan expected this. Her mother was good at making her feel uncomfortable and Susan and her husband had decided to put having children on the backburner until they were ready to be parents. Instead of answering in a bitter way, Susan understood her mother's need to feel validated. "Oh, mom," she answered. "You told me never to have kids until I was old enough and responsible enough. That time will come."

Socially, you need to be happy in yourself and learn to interact with people in a positive way. The moment you let people get under your skin is the moment you stop being authentic and start role-playing to please others. Stop it. Learn that these social gatherings are about making your stamp on the people you meet as a very happy and healthy individual who is authentic and isn't afraid of being him/herself.

Conclusion

Whatever happens in your life will affect the way that you feel about yourself. You need to learn to look at mistakes in a very different way. If you make mistakes, don't judge yourself for them. Instead, learn something from them and then move on. During this book, we have taught you how to recognize which part of you is authentic and which part bends to please other people.

We have given you exercises to try and improve the way that you look at your life and to help you to build up your self-confidence. Throughout the course of the book, you have learned how others can influence your level of happiness if YOU let them. However, we have given you alternatives and there are always alternatives. We have taught you to use mindfulness to get rid of all those negative thoughts. We have also taught you to stop holding yourself back from life by holding onto souvenirs of your failings in life.

You are a very valuable human being. There are probably areas that you need to go over before you start your 30-day journey from where you are now to where you need to be. Understand the implications. Understand how it all depends upon your approach and your ability to follow through. We have given you examples of situations like yours where people have overcome difficulties and these are to help you to find solutions to problems you currently find too difficult to cope with.

Self-love is important. If you can love yourself, people find you easier to love as equals. You won't have to deal with inequality in friendships. You won't have to keep changing who you are to suit different people. What you will find is that people will be attracted toward you because of who you are, rather than who you pretend to be. Stop pretending and let the real you emerge. When you do, your life begins and you will find that self-love is the first step toward happiness.

Help me improve this book

While I have never met you, if you made it through this book I know that you are the kind of person that is wanting to get better and is willing to take on tough feedback to get to that point. You and I are cut from the same cloth in that respect. I am always looking to get better and I wish to not just improve myself, but also this book. If you have positive feedback, please take the time to leave a review. It will help other find this book and it can help change a life in the same way that it changed yours. If you have constructive feedback, please also leave a review. It will help me better understand what you, the reader, need to make significant improvements in your life. I will take your feedback and use it to improve this book so that it can become more powerful and beneficial to all those who encounter it.

http://viewbook.at/selflove

REMEMBER TO JOIN THE GROUP NOW!

If you have not joined the Mastermind Self Development group yet, now is your time! You will receive videos and articles from top authorities in self development as well as a special group only offers on new books and training programs. There will also be a monthly member only draw that gives you a chance to win any book from your Kindle wish list!

If you sign up through this link http://www.mastermindselfdevelopment.com/specialreport you will also get a special free report on the Wheel of Life. This report will give you a visual look at your current life and then take you through a series of exercises that will help you plan what your perfect life looks like. The workbook does not end there; we then take you through a process to help you plan how to achieve that perfect life. The process is very powerful and has the potential to change your life forever. Join the group now and start to change your life! http://www.mastermindselfdevelopment.com/specialreport

You will also love these other great titles from Mastermind Self Development!

You will want to check out these other great titles Mastermind Self Development. All available in the Kindle store or you can just click on covers below.

mybook.to/positivethink

getBook.at/tonyrobbins

You can also find these titles by searching them in the Kindle store on Amazon.

www.ingramcontent.com/pod-product-compliance
Lightning Source LLC
Chambersburg PA
CBHW081412070526
44583CB00020B/2780